ACRL ACTIVE GUIDE

Pay It Forward:
Mentoring New Information Professionals

MARY ANN MAVRINAC
KIM STYMEST

Association of College and Research Libraries
A Division of the American Library Association
Chicago 2012

ACRL ACTIVE GUIDES

Active Guides is an occasional series published by ACRL. They provide a focused exploration of a given topic. Each guide highlights a workplace issue facing library professionals and offers both a theoretical perspective and several practical applications. The theoretical perspective examines an approach, model, or specific tool related to the issue and will lay the groundwork for the applications.

Other guidebooks currently available include:

Life-Work Balance
Conversations that Work
Influencing without Authority

TABLE OF CONTENTS

Chapter 1
INTRODUCTION

One of the most rewarding parts of my job—well my profession—is the opportunity to meet and work with new information professionals. Whether it's guest lecturing in a graduate class, critiquing resumes and cover letters, meeting to discuss career aspirations or a full blown mentoring partnership, each interaction is fulfilling, rewarding and, quite simply, feels good. These interactions provide me the opportunity to encapsulate my professional role, discuss how I got to where I am, share professional values, translate culture, tacit knowledge and the political environment, and most importantly, gain an insight into the lives of a younger generation, a generation who will carry our profession forward in future years.

New information professionals are interested in the combination of serendipity and opportunity seeking that result in jobs and career advancement. They cannot imagine how we got to where we are when they are trying to land their first full time job. I have a vivid memory of sitting in a graduate class when a working professional addressed our class. I was in awe, and thought, "Wow! Will I ever have a position like that? Will I ever be so confident? How did she get that job?" I was riddled with a mixture of awe and excitement; to me, the guest lecturer, was a role model to which to aspire.

As a new information professional I did not think to ask anyone to be my mentor. I more or less muddled along in my career, benefitting from the many "good souls" and bosses who helped me at every turn. I think now how much more intentional and reflective my career path might have been had I availed myself the opportunity to work with one or multiple mentors intentionally, with goals in mind. Unlike my mentoring partner and co-author, Kim Stymest, who knows the value of a mentoring partnership, Kim sought me out shortly after she graduated, asking me if I would consider forming a mentoring relationship with her. Kim taught me a valuable lesson: multiple mentors at every stage in our careers is a very wise investment both personally, and for the profession-at-large.

New graduates and new information professionals are, for the most part, trying to get that first full time job that will set them on their career path. Their future lies ahead of them, a blank but urgent canvas: how will I pay my bills much less my student loans if I do not have a job? Is this job going to help or hurt my career? It is a mystery to new information professionals how headship positions are achieved much less having an interest in these positions at all which is a concern for the profession at large. Who will fill these positions when the baby-boomers retire? What was the career path that led someone to obtain their "dream job"? How did she get to where she is today? With this mystery and uncertainty, comes anxiety and doubt for the new information professional.

How can a more seasoned information professional be of assistance? Do we not remember our early career hits and misses? Do we not remember the early contract jobs where we lived from job to job? Do we not remember the anxiety in charting our career path? Like me, did we chart at all? And yet, somehow, we finally landed the job that set us on our way. How did this happen? Was it luck? (Lots of times it was.) We need not leave this to fate. We can pay it forward by contributing to a new information professional's success by entering into a mentoring partnership.

Interacting with new information professionals is fun. It's rewarding. And, it's a professional responsibility that ought to be considered A CALLING! Every contact with a new information professional is a way to connect "us" with "them" in order to assist in navigating the foggy path that is his or her future career, a career that will be their contribution to our profession. Forming a mentoring partnership will be one of the best things you can do for yourself and for our profession. How might this occur? How can we get you involved?

Meet Kim Stymest—new information professional and Mary Ann Mavrinac—seasoned information professional. Through this Active Guide, *Pay it Forward: Mentoring New Information Professionals*, we will bring to you our "voices" to enliven and chart your mentoring partnership.

We will describe the benefits to each partner and to the profession in forming a mentoring partnership. We will provide helpful tips, a tool-kit and insight that will, hopefully, encourage new information professionals to seek out mentoring partners and to compel more seasoned information professionals to heed their professional calling and engage with new information professionals in a mentoring relationship! In fact, this Active Guide is a result of our mentoring partnership. After initial meetings and discussions, we charted our course as mentoring partners, and have never looked back. This has culminated in sharing our experiences in writing this Guide to urge you to "pay it forward."

We have organized this Guide from the philosophical premise upon which our partnership stands—a democratic approach to mentoring—and other important tenets which serve to address the benefits and pitfalls that can befall a mentoring relationship. The mentoring partnership we espouse is situated in the here and now, where multiple mentors are encouraged throughout your career, including those for the seasoned information professional! Read on, then pay it forward!

Reflection Question	
Seasoned Information Professional	**New Information Professional**
List the mentors that you have had in your career and reflect on how these relationships came about. Describe what made the relationship valuable.	*Think of someone you admire, someone that you think of as a role model. This could be someone in the profession, someone famous, alive or deceased. List the person and the qualities that you believe make them admirable.*

Chapter 2
MENTORING: A BRIEF HISTORY IN TIME

Mentoring is an age-old tradition that can be traced back to classical Greece. In *The Iliad and the Odyssey* Odysseus asked his trusted friend Mentor to be a guardian to his son Telemachus during his extended absences while travelling on government business. Mentor became a trusted, wise advisor and protector to Telemachus throughout his life. While fictional, this type of *Mentoring* relationship became the template for the traditional and most popular model of mentoring where a senior person acts as a role model to a junior person, assisting in his/her career and personal development, opening doors and introducing him/her to other influential people.

Telemachus departing from Nestor, painting by Henry Howard (1769–1847)

The complexities of modern work life exacerbated by the pace of change, especially changes in information and communications technology, suggest that we look beyond the one-to-one mentoring relationship between the sage senior person and new junior person. Who could be experienced in all facets of professional life to adequately mentor someone throughout his/her career? A variety of mentoring relationships might be a more robust approach to meet one's many and varied needs. The concept of "multiple mentors" is encouraged in this Guide. No longer do mentoring relationships need to occur solely within one's organization. They can occur irrespective of time and place, widening an individual's learning context. The only limitations are the practical elements of time and available mentors and the 'fear factor': the fear of rejection that a mentoring relationship request might be spurned. Fear not! This Active Guide will help with the nuts and bolts and psychological barriers in forming productive mentoring relationships.

There are a myriad of mentoring types that have evolved since classical Greek times. Multiple mentors can assist in meeting a variety of individual needs which can be short-term or long-term and defined. These can include peer mentoring, co-mentoring, developmental alliances, situational or spot mentoring, "mentoring up" and e-mentoring, to name a few. For the person being mentored, mentoring has moved away from a passive to an active process of self-discovery upon which individuals embark to forge their career path. Dynamic mentoring relationships are often synergistic, characterized by a process of co-learning and co-discovery by each party.

The kind of mentoring being discussed in this Guide is one where an individual seeks a variety of "mentoring partnerships" throughout her/his career. Mentoring partnerships are based upon democratic principles where both parties are equal with each gaining benefit from the mentoring relationship. A mentoring partnership doesn't obviate the need for an early career professional to form a partnership with a more senior colleague; however, it does work best when this relationship is devoid of hierarchy, in particular hierarchy from a direct reporting relationship.

Chapter 3
WE'RE A LEARNING PROFESSION! DEVELOP YOUR PASSION FOR LEADERSHIP

There are all sorts of benefits to both mentoring partners in the course of a mentoring relationship which we will outline in a later chapter. One benefit bears discussion on its own. This is the central role that learning plays in the mentoring partnership. Really? Mentoring is a learning process? Yes! It is fundamentally a learning process, one that is learner-centered, bi-directional and one-to-one.

The context within which librarians and information professionals work is dynamic, ever-changing, fast-paced, technological, and customer-focused. The pace of change is riveting, and one of the main reasons we advocate adoption of a multiple mentor model throughout one's career. Where it took thousands of years before a major technological change took place—for example, from writing to the codex, 4,300 years; from the codex to movable type, 1,150 years; from movable type to the Internet, 524 years; from the Internet to search engines, 19 years; from search engines to Google, 7 years—transformational change will likely occur every 3-5 years from now on, or even faster![1]

How do we keep abreast in this fast-paced, sometimes volatile, environment? Who can know it all? Well, quite simply, no one can but that doesn't stop us from being anxious about staying on top of new technology, inventions, customer demands, and our over-filled inbox. Adopting a multiple mentor model will go a long way towards settling our anxiety about change; but let's tease out the central tenet of mentoring, which is learning. In this fast-paced, ever-changing environment, becoming a "perpetual learner," as coined by organizational theorist and consultant Edgar H. Schein, would put us in a perpetual learning state-of-mind. As Schein states, " we basically do not know what the world of tomorrow will be like except that it will be different."[2]

When we consider that learning *is,* at its most basic, change, this goes a long way towards taking the edge off the trepidation one feels with change and the pace of change. By putting ourselves in the driver's seat and adopting a perpetual learning mode philosophy, each of us can view learning (change) as the natural and normal process that, it is. Proactively and intentionally seeking out mentors when we have aspirations and challenges we wish to productively and mindfully embrace, places mentoring as a central learning process in our professional lives.

Another facet of this that we'd like to introduce is the concept of leadership—leadership that is non-hierarchical, shared, and empowering. Leadership is the process of influencing change. Who better to begin embracing the development of leadership skills than new information professionals in a mentoring (learning) partnership? The mentoring partnership provides an environment to explore leadership concepts, discuss leadership opportunities, and hopefully, sparking an appetite for pursuing leadership positions in one's organization. Through the process of reflective learning, new information professionals can develop into reflective leaders.

As information professionals, learning is a natural "fit" because we're a learning profession! Learning is one of our professional values.[3] As a profession, we support a learning society and lifelong learning. Let's wholly embrace this professional value in our own professional development, utilizing a centuries old learning process that can be tailor-made to each of our learning aspirations. We invite you to include learning and leadership development into your mentoring partnership conversations.

ACTIVITY

Use your list of possible mentors from the Introduction to help you find a mentoring match! Look at the Reflection Questions below to help you determine what characteristics and values will be important to you in your mentoring partnership. This should help you to focus on what you are looking for.

Reflection Questions

In which areas do I wish to develop?

_____

_____

_____

_____

What are my strengths?

_____

_____

_____

_____

In what am I interested but feel I do not have the experience to embrace?

_____

_____

_____

_____

See Appendix 1 for the Leadership Focuser[4] tool that will help you chart your career path over the next several years.

Notes

1. Darnton, Robert. "The Library in the New Age." *The New York Review of Books*, June 12, 2008.

2. Schein, Edgar H. *Organizational Culture and Leadership*. San Francisco: Jossey-Bass, 361.

3. American Library Association, "Core Values Task Force II Report (2004)." American Library Association. http://www.ala.org/aboutala/sites/ala.org.aboutala/files/content/governance/policymanual/updatedpolicymanual/ocrpdfofprm/40-1corevalues.pdf.

4. Form adapted from Lifetime Focuser Quinton International Inc.®

Chapter 4
LEARNING ABOUT SELF

If you are contemplating a mentoring partnership, it is very likely you are interested in leadership or in becoming a leader. Leadership starts with "self"—that is, learning about yourself through self-awareness, self-reflection, and coaching, feedback and mentoring. Why is an understanding of "self" so important in the mentoring partnership, and in your career?

Our sense of "self" defines each of us, our inner essence that encompasses the psychological, moral, ethical, developmental, passionate, intellectual, virtuous and emotional being. Self relates to what drives us: our aspirations, anxieties, beliefs, fears, wants, needs, values, and motivations. Self is who we are and what we do in acting and reacting to life and the world around us. Our self is dynamic and is engaged with itself, others, and its environment.

It follows that our view and understanding of our self will have an important contribution to our professional development, our careers, and how we engage in our mentoring partnership. Are we open to the exploration of our behaviors, fears, wants and needs or are we more closed, more protective, or defensive? Do we typically look to blame others or do we look inward? Do we reflect upon our actions, our inhibitions, or our fears and anxieties and try to adopt new patterns of behavior? Do we know our strengths and what we naturally like to do? What makes us bounce out of bed each morning?

Knowing yourself is a foundational element of authentic leadership. And, knowing yourself will go a long way towards enjoying an authentic mentoring partnership. Remember, mentoring is a learning process. Learning about self is an important step in the mentoring relationship.

Self-awareness and self-perception of our behavior, in particular, the impact of our behavior on others are important elements of being a reflective leader. Building effective relationships are often predicated upon our understanding of self. It follows that our ability to form effective relationships is critical to our success in the workplace and as leaders.

A mentoring relationship provides a unique opportunity to explore topics of self-awareness and self-perception in a supportive environment. Behavioral tendencies that cause us angst can be deconstructed in relation to work situations; these can be discussed in relation to the opportunities and barriers each might contribute or be a barrier to our career aspirations. Comfort with receiving and providing feedback can be developed, contributing positively to our career development. And of course, our openness and receptiveness to feedback in the mentoring partnership provide a barometer to how we might respond to feedback at work.

Good news! There are lots of tools available for mentoring partners to learn about self. Some are self-administered; some require administration and interpretation by a qualified facilitator. We encourage you to review these tools and select one or two that each of you will use. Share and discuss the findings during one of your meetings. This will lead to:

- ✓ Insight into each other's natural strengths and predilections
- ✓ Strengthening the mentoring partnership
- ✓ A process of reflective leadership—essential in being a successful leader
- ✓ Deeper conversations; deeper insight
- ✓ A richer set of goals for the mentoring partnership.

Here are a few tools to get you started.

StrengthsFinder Profile[1]

- an online assessment that provides insight into your natural talents

- will assist you in applying your strengths to leadership awareness and development

Campbell Leadership Descriptor[2]

- developed by the Center for Creative Leadership, it identifies characteristics for essential leadership, some that can be delegated, others that cannot

Myers-Briggs Type Indicator[3]

- measures your psychological preferences in how you perceive the world and how you make decisions
- requires a trained facilitator to administer and debrief the instrument

Kolbe A[4]

- focuses on your natural inclinations and strengths, measuring what you will likely do not what you want to do

DISC Assessment[5]

- personal assessment of your behavioral preferences
- benefits from a trained facilitator

Notes
1. StrengthsFinder. Clifton StrengthsFinder. www.Strengthsfinder.com
2. Center for Creative Leadership. "Campbell Leadership Descriptor: Overview." Center for Creative Leadership. www.ccl.org/leadership/assessments/CLDOverview.aspx
3. Myers-Briggs Type Indicator. CPP, Mountain View, CA. https://www.cpp.com/products/mbti/index.aspx. See also: Myers, Isabel Briggs *Introduction to Type: A Guide to Understanding your Results on the MBTI Instrument*. Mountain View, CA: CPP, Inc, 1998.
4. Kolbe Corp. "Kolbe & You" Kolbe.com. www.kolbe.com
5. Inscape Publishing. "Looking for DiSC Profiles?" DiSC Assessments. www.discprofile.com

Chapter 5
BRIDGING THE MENTORING GAP

Mentoring can mean a number of things. What we are focusing on is the democratic partnership of mentoring that, hopefully, we have inspired you to create. We have told you that this publication came out of our own mentoring partnership.

But what does "mentoring" mean to a new information professional? What is the new information professional's interest in mentoring? We have suggested that the mentoring partnership is about learning, growth and professional development, particularly in areas of leadership. In a later chapter, we also will explain the difference between mentoring and coaching, and how we can allow room for both in the partnership. This chapter's focus is on the gap that can occur between the new information professional and the seasoned information professional in a formalized mentoring partnership, and provides a strategy to help bridge this gap.

I am very fortunate in my early career to have a mentor. Mary Ann and I have been working together in a formal mentoring partnership since a few months after my graduation in 2010. This formal partnership has been integral to my first years of work experience.

I don't consider her my only mentor. Other mentoring *relationships* (and I purposely use the word relationship here, rather than partnership) are informal; the "mentors" in most cases would probably not see themselves as mentors. I am speaking of others in my networks: colleagues and friends. These are the people I have turned to upon occasion when tasked with totally new responsibilities at work, or when asked research questions outside of my expertise; their assistance and support has been a strong contributing factor to my happiness and success at work.

Before writing this chapter, I spent considerable time thinking whether these relationships really played a role *mentoring* my career. I consulted with Mary Ann. She recommended that I read "Reconceptualizing Mentoring at Work: A developmental network perspective."[1] (This is something that we have included in our mentoring partnership agreement: the recommendation of new and helpful readings!). Higgins and Kram discuss the idea of "developmental networks" in which an individual must rely upon multiple people throughout her/his career for developmental support. "An individual's developmental network is a subset of his or her entire social network (cf. Burf, 1992); it does not consist of *all* of an individual's interpersonal relationships, nor does it comprise everyone with whom the protégé ever communicates about development" (Higgins and Kram, 2001, p. 268). Let's, then, call these "informal mentoring relationships" that I mentioned previously, "developmental networks."

As new professionals we often go into new positions, of course excited, but also anxious and somewhat apprehensive. I know I was. Did I know enough? Was I ready? What do real work/world expectations look like? Drawing from the experiences of others, our networks are integral to our success and development in the profession.

We are not only going in nervous, I think that we are also going in ready for new challenges. Right? We are a *learning profession*! This is what unites us!

But, we are new. We *are* still learning. We are developing our professional identity, as well as the new skills that our positions require. I believe that a lot of new information professionals are expecting to do some of this learning through formal, or informal, mentoring partnerships in their first positions, but are maybe not recognizing the importance that developmental networks can play. It is important that the new information professional recognize this and asks those they have identified earlier as possible formal mentors: will you be my mentor?. Whether they are asking individuals that have forged the path ahead of them questions that will offer direction and guidance in their new careers (as a new academic business librarian, I often turned to a friend of mine from school that graduated ahead of me who was also an academic business librarian), or asking an experienced information professional for career guidance and a formal mentoring partnership, it must be the new information professional that initiates the partnership. And no one will initiate it for you.

ACTIVITY:

In previous chapters, we have asked you to list past mentors, or people you admire, and then determine the characteristics and qualities that made these people/relationships valuable to you. You have learned about yourself, and have the resources to move forward with getting to know yourself better. Now, we would like you to list the people, or even potential people, in your developmental network; thinking about who to ask, and what you would ask of them. Be sure to include possibilities for both formal and informal relationships, linking these to your career aspirations.

_____

_____

_____

_____

_____

_____

_____

Note

1.   Higgins, Monica C. and Kram, Kathy E. "Reconceptualizing mentoring at work: A developmental network perspective," *The Academy of Management Review* 26, no. 2, 29.

Chapter 6
THE MENTORING PARTNERSHIP: IT'S CAPACITY BUILDING!

A mentoring partnership, as said, is a learning process. But more, those who seek out mentoring processes are proactively taking responsibility for their learning and development. Engaging with a potential mentoring partner is an opportunity-seeking action—not opportunistic!—seeking opportunity to grow and develop in our career. Mentoring is different than coaching; it focuses on one's career aspirations not on one's day-to-day performance issues, opportunities and challenges.[1] This chapter will focus on the opportunities (and some of the pitfalls) in selecting a mentor that ensure it is capacity building and not capacity limiting.

Most library organizations do not have a formal mentoring program in spite of many good intentions; while others have no intention of developing such a program. Mentoring programs are resource-intensive, need someone to manage and track the process and program, and require a certain "economy of scale" to be effective. As such, formal mentoring programs are beyond the capacity of many organizations. This need not be a deterrent in building our own mentoring partnerships. We believe the most effective mentoring partnerships are comprised of partners from different organizations; however, with an understanding of the potential pitfalls, one can also form a mentoring partnership within one's organization.

People who seek out a mentoring partner are, in essence, building capacity to more fully assume their professional roles: capacity building on an individual, departmental, organizational and professional level. Each builds upon and each contributes to the other. Learning is a capacity building process where, over time, new behaviors, relationships, strategies, skills and abilities are developed. Mentoring is a learning strategy that builds capacity two-by-two with both partners benefiting from the relationship; and in turn, one's departmental unit, organization and the broader profession can benefit. That is the power of capacity building. We'll return to the other benefits of mentoring in a later chapter! What are a few things to keep in mind about the capacity-building nature of a mentoring relationship?

Mary Ann is my first mentor; a partnership that has proven invaluable to me in my career so far. I love librarianship. I went into the field because I wanted to help people. I like to read. I like to research. I like to write. It seemed a logical, if not inevitable step. I did not expect to be blown away by the profession; the passion that so many librarians and information professionals have for it. I did not expect to make so many friends and outstanding connections.

Finding a mentor was important to me, especially when I first graduated, because I knew I had goals. I also knew that I didn't understand how to reach them. I almost felt like the one class missing at library school was "Career Trajectory 101." I had taken advantage of a lot of the opportunities afforded me when I entered library school. I got involved. I made connections (as I have said), but how I might reach my career goals wasn't covered.

So I asked people. My default question when meeting other information professionals was "how did you get to where you are?" More often than not, the story was very similar to what Mary Ann described in the introductory chapter. The problem that I see with this approach is that there are so many new information professionals graduating. How do you make your mark amongst so many eager, talented, colleagues? I don't believe that new information professionals have the luxury anymore of allowing their career paths to just happen to them. We have to take ownership of our careers. We have to set goals. We need to achieve these goals by planning the steps that will help us get there. Mentoring, and capacity building, are two powerful helpmates in helping us achieve our goals and grow as professionals.

As Mary Ann pointed out, there are some things to keep in mind about the capacity-building nature of a mentoring partnership. This is primarily related to determining the appropriate person to approach to be your mentor. What are these things to keep in mind? We believe that the foundation of the mentoring partnership should be based in open and frank communication. This is key to a successful mentoring partnership.

Consider your reporting manager or direct supervisor as a mentor: there will be many things that could come up, in terms of both mentoring and coaching, that you would not want to discuss with your supervisor. This does not preclude the importance of establishing an effective communication pattern and coaching relationship with your supervisor, but this communication would take on a different form in a supervisory role. In a mentoring partnership, this would be "capacity limiting" because you would be limited in your ability to speak freely. The relationship that you have with your supervisor is a formal one that hinges on different roles and responsibilities.

Now consider an organizational member, and colleague, that is *not* your reporting manager. Take, for example, Mike and Suzy who are colleagues in the same organization, and let's say that they are in a mentoring partnership. This type of situation might be "capacity limiting" if some difficulty comes up at work where both people in the mentoring partnership are involved. Let's say that Mike, as the new information professional, is having difficulty navigating a tricky relationship with another colleague, but this colleague happens to work closely with Suzy, his mentor. This type of situation might close one of the key elements of openness, honesty or trust for a successful mentoring partnership, and it then becomes "capacity limiting." You would want in your mentoring partnership the ability to discuss anything that comes up in your career.

Finally, consider someone unrelated to your organization. This creates capacity building because both partners can be open and honest, without concern for issues arising in the workplace.

ACTIVITY:

In this chapter we've identified the things to keep in mind for capacity building, now take your list from the last chapter of possible mentors and determine their appropriateness in the table below. Next list the possible pros and cons that might come up during the course of your mentoring partnership.

	Who	Pros	Cons
• Reporting relationship			
• Within organization • No reporting relationship			
• Non-organizational member			

Notes

1.   See Chapter 10 for a discussion about the difference between mentoring and coaching.

Chapter 7
MYTHS AND FEARS ABOUT MENTORING

It seems such a simple question: *Would you be my mentor?* But in the eyes of the new professional, this question can be anything but simple and there seem to be some major concerns keeping the new professional from asking. I know that I had a number of them. Eventually, I bit the bullet and I just asked.

The first thing that I would beg the more experienced professional to remember is that, those of us who might approach them as potential mentors are new. Being new often goes hand-in-hand with, at least, a small dose of insecurity: in one's abilities, skills and experience. A new information professional will often place a more seasoned professional on a pedestal, particularly, if they are looking to the experienced professional as a possible mentor. This can make asking even more difficult in the eyes of the new professional.

Among the more common beliefs standing in the way of the new professional seeking a mentor might be:

Am I going to look too pushy?	*Are there any other fears you can think of? Write them down.*
Am I too NEW for mentoring?	
I don't want to waste your time!	
This person probably won't have the time.	
I don't know who to ask.	
How do I meet possible mentors?	

Now let's address some of these concerns:

Am I going to look too pushy? In my experience, there is definitely a fine line between being "pushy" and being "keen." I believe that if you maintain your authenticity, friendliness, and are generally nice, you will be perceived as keen or "eager."

Am I too New for mentoring? One of the purposes of this Guide is to point professionals to the idea that there is no such thing as being "too new for mentoring." Mentoring is a learning process that you will continue to draw upon throughout your career, using it at each and every stage.

The other myths/fears are tricky:

I don't want to waste your time! Admittedly, this one, along with *This person probably won't have the time*, are hard. It's true, you may approach someone that is just too busy, but you won't know until you ask. Chances are, that person will honest with you about whether they can make the time commitment or not. You have more than likely paid them a compliment by finding them worthy of asking.

I don't know who to ask. Knowing who to ask is an important part of the mentoring relationship. One could even argue that knowing who to ask is *the* most important step in establishing a mentoring relationship. It is part knowing your self (tools such as those listed in the chapter on Learning About Self), part knowing where you want to go (tools such as the Leadership Focuser, see Appendix 1), and part building your network (*How do I meet possible mentors?*) (see the Networking exercise in this chapter). These tools should help get you started.

Armed with this knowledge about the myths and fears of forming a mentoring relationship, knowledge about yourself and your goals, and some new networking tricks, will help you bite the bullet.

ACTIVITY
Networking exercise:

There are many ways to grow your network. One way is to ask someone you know and trust to recommend someone for you to talk to. Ask this person for some of his or her time (maybe over coffee). When you wrap up your conversation with him/her, asking them to recommend 1 or 2 other people for you to connect with. By using this technique, your network will grow.

Are there other ways to expand your network?

_____

_____

_____

_____

_____

_____

_____

_____

_____

_____

Chapter 8
WHAT DO WE DO NOW? PLANNING FOR THE MENTORING PARTNERSHIP

You've gathered the courage. You've asked the question. And you've gotten the answer you were hoping for. You have a mentor. But are you ready to start? Probably not; there are a number of things that you should be thinking of before you begin. Did I know this? No.

I began in my mentoring partnership completely excited to get started and then realized that I didn't really know what we were supposed to do. Wasn't I just supposed to sit back and absorb the wisdom?

Absolutely not.

Mentoring is an active relationship between partners, but the onus is on the new information professional to get things started. You cannot expect your mentor to hold your hand in the process, guiding you through. *You* want this. *You* initiated this. You have the greater responsibility for orienting the relationship and for making clear your goals and needs. And despite the many benefits that *both* of you will reap, it is your responsibility to do the work.

I was asked to set goals. These goals were of two kinds: goals that were for my development (what I wanted to achieve in my career) and goals for the mentoring partnership. The latter took into account what I wanted to achieve from the partnership, or to put it another way, what I wanted us to work on.

This was hard for me, but it really forced me to look at what I wanted and where I wanted to go with my career. It forced me to look, realistically, at when I wanted to accomplish the things that I want to accomplish.

Considering what I wanted out of the partnership was even harder. This brought up some of my fears again. Will she agree to what I want out of the partnership? I discovered that I wouldn't know if I didn't ask.

After a time of researching and soul-searching, I made sure in my lengthy list that I sent out for approval—it was important to us that my goals be mutually agreed upon—to include in my goals that my mentor be proud of the relationship. I felt that this was really important. For the same reason I also had listed that we periodically check in with each other to determine whether or not the partnership was still working; whether or not it was still beneficial, and if so, if the benefit was still mutual?

Mary Ann is now going to provide some tips and ideas on setting ground rules before you begin, as well as what to think about in terms of goals and structure.

Thanks, Kim.

Any successful partnership begins with an agreed upon structure and plan. A mentoring partnership is no different. Providing a structure to support the mentoring partnership clarifies roles, expectations and rules of the game, including the "nitty-gritty" such as the frequency and length of meetings. It also goes a long way towards ensuring it will be mutually beneficial to both parties.

It is ideal if at least the first mentoring meeting occur in person, especially for mentoring partnerships that will occur at a distance. Developing rapport and comfort between the mentoring partners is an essential element that cannot be rushed. If this is a relatively new relationship, the first meeting can help to establish the tone of the mentoring relationship. The partners will fall into a relationship pattern that establishes a tone that, over time will likely change, but at least in the beginning, the first meeting can inform the approach that will be taken during subsequent meetings.

It is important that the first few meetings and all subsequent meetings focus on building the relationship so that trust is established and continues to develop. Mentoring relationships are enriched when there is comfort in talking about personal, emotional, and sometimes revealing, topics where one's vulnerabilities emerge. An open, nurturing mentoring partnership is a privilege born out of humility that each partner should respect and cherish. The goal of a successful partnership is for each partner to ask: how might I be of assistance? How might I be supportive?

What are some of the necessary elements of a structure that supports the mentoring partnership?

Ground Rules:

✓ Establish ground rules: Will all conversations be deemed confidential or will there be an agreed upon commitment that, when a topic is confidential, it is stated up front? What are the responsibilities of each person?

✓ Model the way: Mentors play an important role in "modeling the way." All conversations should be respectful, including topics which are emotionally pitched. The mentoring discussion is a great time to practice professional discourse and behavior in a safe environment. Use role playing to strategize on effective ways to tackle thorny issues.

✓ Anonymity: It is a "must" that discussions about co-workers, supervisors or others be anonymous in as much as this is possible. Remember: it is easy to quickly form and share and opinion; it is more difficult to show restraint. Aim the bar high. Discuss strategy and context not individuals and personality.

Goals and Structure:

✓ Establish goals: Each party should prepare his/her individual goals for the mentoring partnership. The more specific the goals the better! Include time lines for each. This will help manage expectations and mitigate disappointment.

✓ Agree Upon Goals: review each other's goals. Discuss, make necessary changes and agree upon the goals. Celebrate! You're ready to go!

✓ Meetings—establish the frequency and length of meetings. Will these take place in person or otherwise? Be open to the need for meetings to occur outside the cycle when pressing matters emerge

✓ Agendas—prepare an agenda for meetings to ensure topics are known in advance and adequate time allotted for each. How far in advance will the agenda be sent? (Remember to place coaching topics at the beginning!)* See Chapter 10 for a discussion about mentoring and coaching.

Chapter 9
MENTORING NEW INFORMATION PROFESSIONALS FOR MANAGEMENT AND LEADERSHIP

I remember the first day of my mandatory first year management class during my masters and thinking "what am I doing here? Why do I have to take this class?" I did not have any interest in becoming a manager. So much so, in fact, that when the professor asked her introductory questions:

"Who here wants to be a manager one day?" I did not raise my hand; not many people in the class did. She followed the question up with: *"Who is interested in being a leader?"*

She got a few more hands raised on this one, but probably fewer than half of the class responded.

Let me begin by saying that I no longer feel this avoidance about management and leadership. But this initial hesitation from students and new information professionals is a major problem for librarianship. Like many professions these days, librarianship will be facing a rising number of retirements in the coming years. In the United States, the research suggests similar concerns; the American Library Association's study *Planning for 2015: The Recent History and Future Supply of Librarians* offers projections on the number of retirements and the number of librarians expected in 2015.[1] In Canada the most recent research foresees a major upcoming crisis with the number of retirements exceeding incoming new and current librarians.[2]

There is a need for new information professionals to step into management roles, possibly, earlier than anticipated. And in some cases, people will wind up in management when they are *still* not interested in being in a manager.

35

Clearly, these are problems.

Now these questions that my professor asked raise interesting questions. Do we really understand what management and leadership are? What is a manager? What is management? What is a leader? What is leadership? Here are a few definitions for you to consider.

> Management: an authority relationship between at least two people governed by organizational policy, rewards and punishment, the purpose of which is to achieve organizational outcomes through the processes of planning, budgeting, staffing, organizing, problem-solving and evaluating processes.

> Leadership: a relationship of influence between at least two people, not necessarily related to position, who strive towards a shared purpose that results in meaningful and substantive change that benefits both parties and the organization. The influence process may be persuasive, but it is not coercive.[3]

I think that we, as new information professionals, often sell ourselves short. We often have some experience with leadership or management, but we often believe that our experiences *outside* of librarianship don't count toward our experiences *inside* librarianship, i.e. we discount our experiences in student government, or sports team leadership, or supervisory experience in, perhaps, retail, or volunteer positions. These are simple examples of both leadership and management, in contexts that we might discount because they are outside of librarianship. I would like to argue, however, that it is these experiences that make for better information professionals, for more well-rounded librarians, for professionals that understand context.

One of the many benefits to our diverse educational and working backgrounds is the transferable skills that we bring to our new environments, but I think that we are too often nervous about seeing the transferability of these skills! Maybe new information professionals are worried about making a 'hard sell' of some of those skills; I know I was. I was worried that my work experience prior to library school didn't really count. But, I ran my own business for a year, and now I find that I have some relevant stories from this time in my life that are relatable to new business students in my library. I have relevant work experience and stories to pull from during interviews. It's about transferable skills; and it's about bringing everything that you have to the table. And it's about developing new skills as well.

Reflection Questions

Do these definitions resonate with you? Do they change your mind? How would you define a "manager"?

_____

_____

_____

How would you define a "leader"?

_____

_____

_____

Think of someone that you feel is a good "manager"; a good "leader." Note four key words that make them stand out!

_____

_____

_____

_____

What about someone who is a great manager or a great leader? Note four key words that make them stand out!

_____

_____

_____

_____

What might interest you in management or in leadership?

_____

_____

_____

What transferable skills do you have in the areas of management and leadership?"

_____

_____

_____

Some other questions for you to consider: What thoughts, fears, opportunities, and challenges do you, as a new information professional, perceive about supervision? What myths do you carry? Is it about not wanting to do a performance evaluation; is it the "hassle" in managing people? Give some thought to these questions; your answers might help you shed some light on why you *would* like to be in a leadership or management role.

We would suggest that new information professionals can work with their mentors and their workplace supervisors to identify opportunities to obtain supervisory and management training. Far too many people enter these roles without ever having any training. Remember, we're a learning profession. Who would enter a supervisory role without having learned some basics on what it takes to be an effective supervisor or manager? A few friends of mine from library school have found themselves in management roles early in their careers. Some have simply transitioned to these roles with help from peers and networks. Others have really struggled. Some could use a mentor.

We believe that you can be a fairly effective supervisor/manager without being a leader; however, you cannot be an effective leader without being an effective manager. Mentoring can assist in developing the qualities of leadership, and can, therefore, help in building better managers. What I mean is that through the mentoring partnership, leadership can be nurtured and developed at any stage and amongst any group regardless of hierarchy. I think we can probably all agree that our profession has always needed, and will continue to need, leaders!

With this in mind, I think that it's probably important to know what people are looking for in a good leader. You have some of your own ideas from the reflection questions. Leadership authors and experts, James Kouzes and Barry Posner describe four qualities of a leader: honesty, a forward-looking approach, someone who is inspiring and someone who is competent.[4] Leadership qualities can often be learned, so don't let this deter you; just have a look at some of the tools that we have suggested in the "Learning About Self" chapter to guide your thoughts.

Further to this, be sure to look for opportunities. There are often leadership opportunities (without being in a specific management role) in our positions. You can start small and build your skills as you go. There are opportunities in associations, organizations, to lead teams or projects, in and out of the workplace. Even being the chair of a social committee at work can provide a great insight into leadership. Taking up these opportunities in your workplace will often be viewed favorably and help to build your resume, as well. These opportunities can often assist in creating the hunger for management opportunities that is also needed in our profession. And you'll have the opportunity to begin paying it forward!

Notes

1. American Library Association. *Planning for 2015: The Recent History and Future Supply of Librarians*. American Library Association. http://www.ala.org/research/files/librarystaffstats/recruitment/Librarians_supply_demog_analys.pdf.

2. University of Alberta. "The Future of Human Resources in Canadian Libraries." *8Rs Canadian Library Human Resources Study*. http://www.ls.ualberta.ca/8rs/8RsFutureofHRLibraries.pdf.

3. Burns, James M. *Leadership*. New York: Harper & Row, 1978.

4. Kouzes, James M. and Posner, Barry Z. *The Leadership Challenge*. San Francisco: Josey-Bass, 2007.

Chapter 10
MENTORING AND COACHING: WHAT'S THE DIFFERENCE?

A mentoring partnership between two information professionals at different stages in their respective careers will inevitably be a mix of mentoring and coaching especially when the relationship is comprised of a new and a seasoned information professional.

Mentoring and coaching share many of the same characteristics: a mutually respectful, trusting relationship where open conversations are encouraged in a safe environment. Both mentoring and coaching are learning processes. Both have a mutual interest in a positive outcome for each party, in particular for the partner who has sought out the relationship with specific goals and outcomes in mind. So, what's the difference between mentoring and coaching? Aren't they one and the same?

Well, not really. Mentoring is typically more holistic in its approach towards the development of another's career aspirations whether short or longer term. This can include a transfer of knowledge, including tacit knowledge, discussions about core values and organizational culture, and exposure to networks to expand another's sphere of relationships.

On the other hand, coaching relationships focus primarily on building performance or addressing performance issues. A coaching relationship is typically short-term in nature and seeks to address a specific work performance issue or need; however, a coaching relationship can also be a longer-term relationship. The key difference is that the focus is on job performance.

Coaching relationships do not usually include mentoring; however, mentoring relationships often include coaching.

Experiencing a mentoring relationship with a new information professional is often a balancing act between coaching and mentoring, especially if the new information professional is in a new job or is experiencing challenging issues or relationships at work. These mentoring relationships will start out with clear, mutually agreed upon goals, and each meeting will be organized with an agenda; however, the entire time devoted to mentoring can be "derailed" if the new information professional has a pressing, often emotional issue related to specific job performance.

It's important to acknowledge coaching as a vital component of the mentoring partnership or else the new information professional might not be able to emotionally focus on his/ her long term career goals and aspirations. There are too many "front of mind" issues that are circling and getting in the way of a strategic conversation on long term career development.

New information professionals are often thrust into extremely challenging positions at work even in entry-level positions. They can be apprehensive about addressing issues with their supervisors, concerned that this will reflect badly upon them if they look like they do not know what they are doing. This vulnerability is exacerbated when the position is on a contract basis.

Supervisors are not always attuned to the "newness" of a new information professional fresh out of school. It is not uncommon for new information professionals to report that their supervisor does not book regular meetings with them. They often feel isolated; they can feel in over their heads. Often the issues at hand would challenge a seasoned professional including inappropriate behaviors such as bullying, unrealistic expectations or communication issues with little orientation or training. This puts the new information professional in a vulnerable position: he/she needs to have a good experience in his/her first job; and a good reference is essential in order to get the next job!

The mentoring relationship can play a vital role.

> ### TIP!
>
> Include an agenda item devoted to current issues or "what's on your mind."
>
> Position this at the beginning of the agenda.
>
> Allot a specific amount of time and negotiate any time beyond that.
>
> Establish ground rules that include:
>
> ✓ A brief outline of topic
> ✓ Prepare possible strategies or solutions beforehand
> ✓ Protect the identity of the protagonists
>
> Ground rules establish expectations for professionalism and decorum during these discussions and model professional behavior that can be used in the workplace to address challenging issues and relationships.

These strategies also go a long way towards reducing anxiety and emotions and depersonalizing the issue. However, it's best to acknowledge and discuss the emotional elements of a topic especially if emotions are running high. These can't be ignored because emotions often drive behaviour. Part of the coaching relationship with new information professionals will be mutually developing strategies for working through emotional issues to ensure that work relationships are not harmed or that irrevocable damage is not done. Why? Because these can harm a new information professional's career, and as such, will have a direct impact on the success and outcome in achieving the goals of the mentoring relationship.

If a new information professional is having difficulty navigating the rocky shoals of a work environment or a particular relationship, he/she will need assistance in order to be successful in his/her career. So don't ignore the powerful pull of coaching. But do provide ground rules for these discussions, insisting upon the use of professional language, professional behavior and a productive discussion of strategies and outcomes. Once discussed, the meeting can move on to the other mentoring agenda items.

ACTIVITY

Try to identify whether the statements and questions below are "mentoring" or "coaching" topics. Then identify some of your own questions or statements.

	Mentoring	Coaching
I want to be a department head	☐	☐
I'm scared to talk to my boss	☐	☐
Which professional associations should I join?	☐	☐
I have new responsibilities and I'm not sure how to do them?	☐	☐
I'm struggling to articulate my vision for libraries	☐	☐
I'm having some trouble getting my ideas heard at meetings	☐	☐
I have been invited to apply for a position in another library but have not been at my current job very long. What should I do?	☐	☐

I'm having a difficult time communicating with a colleague at work.	☐	☐
I would like to move to the next level of training in my job but I don't know how to ask for this.	☐	☐
When people ask me where I see myself in five years I have a hard time answering.	☐	☐

(See following page for answers)

ACTIVITY

Try to identify whether the statements and questions below are "mentoring" or "coaching" topics. Then identify some of your own questions or statements.

	Mentoring	Coaching
I want to be a department head	X	☐
I'm scared to talk to my boss	☐	X
Which professional associations should I join?	X	☐
I have new responsibilities and I'm not sure how to do them?	☐	X
I'm struggling to articulate my vision for libraries	X	☐
I'm having some trouble getting my ideas heard at meetings	☐	X
I have been invited to apply for a position in another library but have not been at my current job very long. What should I do?	X	☐
I'm having a difficult time communicating with a colleague at work.	☐	X
I would like to move to the next level of training in my job but I don't know how to ask for this.	X	☐
When people ask me where I see myself in five years I have a hard time answering.	X	☐

Chapter 11
WHAT'S IN IT FOR ME?

The mentoring partnership is based upon democratic principles where both parties are equal and where each gains from the mentoring relationship. So, from the seasoned information professional's viewpoint: what's in it for *me*? Why would I want to be in a mentoring partnership? I'm too busy as it is! I already have lots of people in my personal network. I'm sick and tired of new graduates thinking they know it all!

To the new professional, I can almost imagine what you might be thinking... Really? There's more? I just finished another degree, I'm looking for a job and you want me to do more work? The good news? I know by now you must be wondering where the good news is. It's incredibly rewarding work that we do. And mentoring can be a part of it.

So, what's it in for me? I am afraid to ask. Who am I to think that someone would want to partner with me, especially if they are mid or late-career? I fear rejection. The myths and fears of forming a mentoring partnership have already been discussed in an earlier chapter. These may persist. Read on! "What's in it for *me*?" may convince you that mentoring partnerships might be the most valuable relationships you form in your career—new, mid or late-career!

Seasoned Information Professional

Pay it Forward
- selflessly assists in the career advancement of new librarians
- gives back to the profession
- it's intrinsically rewarding
- enriches professional life by providing guidance, insight and affirmation to interpret context, translate the political environment and help navigate career progression
- feels good to give back.

Learning
- each partner contributes and learns through the course of the relationship
- gains insight into a younger generation, their educational experiences, job being assumed, and exposure to the entry-level job market
- appreciates the challenges faced in navigating early career milestones
- experiences insight into the opportunities and challenges a new information professional faces
- understands the values, skills and perspective of a younger generation.

Empathy
- inspires an empathic reaction and empathic perspective for the needs of new information professionals
- protects and stands up for them when they are vulnerable
- inspires heightened awareness of the requirements needed to foster success
- triggers a desire to support the next generation of information professionals so they are ready to assume leadership roles.

New Information Professional
Pay it Forward   • learns a spirit of reciprocity   • experiences a seasoned professional giving back to the profession   • motivates you to "pay it forward" to continue the cycle of giving back to the profession.
Learning   • each partner contributes and learns through the course of the relationship   • assists in shaping mentoring and career goals   • learns from the experiences and history of the mentor, including a few "what not to do" lessons.
Empathy   • cultivates sensitivity that new ideas and theories learned in school are sometimes not enough to implement in the workplace   • gains insight into bridging the gap from ideas to implementation to outcomes.

Seasoned Information Professional
Tacit Knowledge   • shares tacit knowledge, the kind of knowledge that's implied and not spoken, but simply is   • translates the culture of the profession.
"Mentoring Up"   • learns from younger colleagues in areas where one is losing ground   • declares vulnerability in a safe relationship to address perceived slippage in staying abreast of trends, technology, attitudes and skills.
Transmitting Values   • implicitly and explicitly transmits values—essential in a values-based profession.
Research and Publishing   • provides opportunities for co-researching and publishing   • transfers knowledge, methods and skills in research and publication   • obtains ideas of and assistance from a new information professional who may have more time to devote to these projects

New Information Professional
Tacit Knowledge <ul><li>learns to speak the language of the profession and knowledge that is not found in a book</li><li>learns about lived experience, a great advantage to the new information professional.</li></ul>
"Mentoring Up" <ul><li>provides opportunity to offer unvarnished opinions, perspectives and ideas</li><li>offers feedback, training and support to the mentoring partner</li><li>bolsters confidence, helps formulate ideas and empowers when you can "mentor up."</li></ul>
Transmitting Values <ul><li>learns and shares values</li><li>evaluates and weighs how these values can be applied in light of changes in the profession, technology and the environment</li><li>learns about the enduring nature of core values.</li></ul>
Research and Publishing <ul><li>obtains insight and an entrée into the world of research and publication</li><li>contributes time and energy to support a more seasoned colleague who may have less time to devote to these projects</li><li>gets published!</li></ul>

Seasoned Information Professional

Capacity Building
- supports the next generation of library and information professional leaders one leader at a time
- contributes to their success through strategic action
- increases the ability and understanding of the new professional
- positively contributes to individual development and that of one's department, organization and the profession at large
- bolsters retention in the profession

New Relationships
- fosters and adds new relationships to one's personal network
- leverages these relationships for future assistance and advice
- cultivates deep, enduring relationships, some which span generations.

Celebrating Success
- it's rewarding and euphoric to celebrate success, especially if the mentoring relationship contributed to this success.

New Information Professional

Capacity Building
- capacity building through the reciprocity of "paying it forward"
- grows the profession and strengthens a network of information professionals that share the same values and vision.

New Relationships
- grows and strengthens your professional network
- provides introductions that you might not otherwise have
- connects you with others that may be better able to provide support in specific areas of your development
- refers you to other new information professionals, providing the opportunity to *pay it forward* early in your career.

Celebrating Success
- exciting and rewarding to hear your mentor say "Woohoo!" when you have landed that position that you wanted so badly!
- celebrating career success with your mentor is truly something special because he/she understands the achievement in a professional context that others may not.

Chapter 12
CONCLUSION

Would you be my mentor?

It felt silly. I can tell you that. I was nervous; I admire her so much. What if she said no? But I wouldn't know if I didn't ask.

In the two years of working together, the mentoring partnership that Mary Ann and I formed has grown and adapted. It has seen a lot of change. And it will continue to as we move to different stages of our careers. This is true for both of us. I will not always be a "new information professional" (though it sometimes seems hard to believe!). And Mary Ann will continue to move in her career, to grow and learn.

This is what mentoring is about.

Whether you are a new information professional, mid- or late-career, we hope you were able to gather some important ideas and steps in the guide. We hope that you will see mentoring, as we do; not just as a static relationship, but as a dynamic, democratic process in which *both* partners benefit. A mentoring partnership can hold so much value for all of those involved and can play such an important role in both parties' careers. As we wrote in an earlier chapter, there may be people who do not think of themselves as mentors but whose importance is significant to one's success and well-being.

Mentoring, as we see it, is a tremendous opportunity in our profession, an opportunity to build upon what we already do so well: we help, we learn and we grow. Mary Ann has told us from the outset that interacting with new information professionals is fun, rewarding and should be considered a professional responsibility, a CALLING!

Forming a mentoring partnership will be one of the best things you can do for yourself and for our profession.

We hope that through our stories, and the questions and activities in which we have engaged you, we have provided you with some fundamental pieces to move forward with a mentoring partnership of your own.

We hope that you will pay it forward.

Appendix 1
LEADERSHIP FOCUSER[1]

Goal:
✓ To derive benefit and growth for yourself and for your organization.

Outcomes:
✓ Leverage your leadership strengths into actions and positive outcomes.

✓ Strengthen your challenges and areas in need of improvement through actions and positive outcomes.

✓ Commit to outcomes through tangible actions starting tomorrow, and then through to one year.

Exercise:
✓ List your leadership strengths and areas in need of improvement.

✓ Select one strength and one area in need of improvement you wish to leverage and develop into tangible outcomes.

✓ Using the form below, start with 1 Year ahead. State specific desired outcomes for your strength and your area in need of improvement.

✓ Go to "Tomorrow." State what you will do **tomorrow** to advance the outcomes you identified at 1 Year.

✓ Continue with 1 Week, then 3 Months, then 6 Months.

Note
1.   Form adapted from Lifetime Focuser Quinton International Inc.®

Leadership Focuser   Date:

1 Year		6 Months	

3 Months		1 Month	

1 Week		Tomorrow	